IS IT
cience?

The Sun and The Earth

Rebecca Stefoff

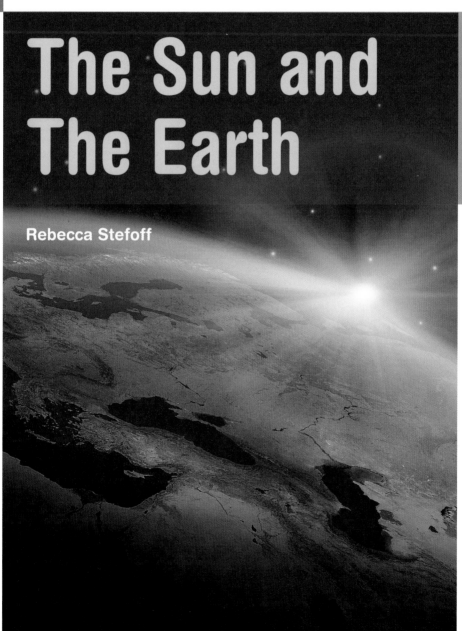

Cavendish
Square

New York

Published in 2014 by Cavendish Square Publishing, LLC
303 Park Avenue South, Suite 1247, New York, NY 10010

Library of Congress Cataloging-in-Publication Data

Stefoff, Rebecca.
The sun and the earth / by Rebecca Stefoff.
  p. cm. — (Is it science?)
Includes index.
ISBN 978-1-62712-521-5 (hardcover) ISBN 978-1-62712-522-2 (paperback) ISBN 978-1-62712-523-9 (ebook)
1.Earth (Planet) — Juvenile literature. 2. Sun — Juvenile literature. I. Stefoff, Rebecca, 1951-. II. Title.
QB631.4 S83 2014
550—dc23

Editorial Director: Dean Miller
Senior Editor: Peter Mavrikis
Copy Editor: Cynthia Roby
Art Director: Jeffrey Talbot
Designer: Amy Greenan
Photo Researcher: Julie Alissi, J8 Media
Production Manager: Jennifer Ryder-Talbot
Production Editor: Andrew Coddington

IS IT
cience?

Contents

The Sun and The Earth

The daily rising and setting of the sun makes it easy to believe that the sun moves around Earth. Discovering the true movements of Earth and the sun is one of science's triumphs.

Going Around or Standing Still

If the building you were standing in moved, you would feel it, wouldn't you? If the ground moved under your feet, you'd feel that, too. You would probably yell, "Earthquake!" But could the whole world move without anyone feeling it?

Four hundred years ago in Europe, people were asking that question because a handful of thinkers and scientists had come up with a startling new idea. Earth, they said, moved around the sun. That idea does not seem strange today, but back then it was shocking. Everyone *knew* that Earth didn't move—it was the sun that moved. You could see it with your own eyes. Each morning the sun rose above the horizon in the east. During the day it traveled across the sky, and when it sank below the horizon in the west, night fell. The sun's path changed positions slowly over the course of each year, but it always stayed within a band of the sky called the **zodiac**.

The night sky moved, too. Between sunset and sunrise, the glittering stars wheeled slowly across the sky from east to west in their fixed patterns. Five other lights moved along the zodiac on courses of their own. These were Mercury, Venus, Mars, Jupiter, and Saturn, the planets that can be seen with the human eye.

People everywhere were familiar with the movements of the sun, moon, planets, and stars. All of these heavenly bodies appeared to **revolve**, or move in a circle, around Earth, which stood still. The idea that Earth could be revolving around the sun, and not the sun around Earth, seemed to go against common sense. But the notion of a moving Earth went against more than just common sense. It also challenged deeply rooted beliefs. In fact, the idea of a moving Earth disturbed people so much that it was dangerous. One of the greatest scientists of the seventeenth century, Galileo Galilei, faced death just for writing about it.

Galilei helped change the way we see the universe. He was one link in the chain of thinkers who turned the old Earth-centered, or **geocentric**, view of the heavens into today's sun-centered, or **heliocentric**, view. The shift away from believing that Earth was the center of the universe was the start of modern **astronomy**, the study of space and everything in it. To understand how this change came about, it helps to know about a powerful tool called the **scientific method**.

ONE

How Science Works

Science is the search for accurate knowledge about the world. Scientists rely on the scientific method, which came into use during the seventeenth century, to guide this search.

The Scientific Method

The scientific method is a process, or series of steps. There are many versions of this method, but the basic steps are:

Observation

Research

Hypothesis

Test or Experiment

Conclusion

Share and Repeat

Observation means seeing something that raises a question. For example, ancient **astronomers** noticed that certain heavenly bodies appear to wander in the sky. These became known as *planets*, from the Greek word *planetes*, meaning "wanderer."

Research means gathering data, or information, that might answer the question. Maybe the answer is already known. If it is not known, research gives the scientist data that may lead to the answer.

To research the movements of the planets thousands of years ago, skywatchers observed them carefully and kept detailed records of their positions against the starry background. Early astronomers became familiar with the planets' movements. They charted and predicted them with great accuracy.

The paths of the planets, as seen from Earth, turned out to be complicated. Each night the planets wheel across the sky from east to west, just like the stars and moon. But sometimes a planet appears to stop in its path, stand still for a few nights, and then move backward (westward) against the stars. This backward motion is called retrograding, or being in **retrograde**. Weeks or months later, the planet stops retrograding and goes back to its normal direction of travel. What could make a planet move forward, backward, and then forward again?

A *hypothesis* is the next step in the scientific method. It is an educated guess based on what the scientist has observed and researched. Different hypotheses for the retrograde movements of the planets were part of the life-or-death struggle between **geo-centrism**, the model of the universe with Earth at the center, and **heliocentrism**, the model with the sun at the center.

Testing the hypothesis shows whether or not it is the right explanation. This part of the scientific method often involves experiments. Even when a scientist cannot actually do a particular experiment, he or she must at least be able to *think* of a way the hypothesis could be tested.

An ancient astronomer could not send a space probe high

Earth and other planets move around the sun in paths called orbits.

above the **solar system** to see whether the sun goes around Earth or Earth goes around the sun. But the astronomer might have thought, "If a person could somehow rise high enough to look down on Earth and sun from above, the question would be answered." A scientific hypothesis must be testable. If it cannot be tested, it cannot be proved or disproved. That takes it out of the realm of science.

One way to test a hypothesis is to ask, "If my hypothesis is correct, what other things must be true, too?" If Earth revolves around the sun, for example, the stars should appear in different parts of the sky when seen from different points in Earth's orbit. This is called **parallax**, the appearance of movement when a distant object is sighted from different viewpoints.

Parallax at the Tip of Your Thumb

You have a simple example of parallax right in your hand. Stretch out one arm and stick up your thumb. Close your left eye. Using only your right eye, line up your thumb with something, like a tree, across the street. Now, without moving your hand, close your right eye and open your left eye. Did the tree "jump" several inches to the left of your thumb? It didn't really move. Neither did your thumb. But the distance between your two eyes created a parallax—a difference in viewpoints that made it *seem* as if the object shifted its position.

In a case that pitted science against religion, Galileo was punished by the Inquisition, a court of the Roman Catholic Church, for supporting the idea that Earth revolves around the sun.

A *conclusion* comes from tests and experiments. In this step, the scientist looks at the results of the experiments and asks, "Do these results support my hypothesis?"

If the answer is "no," the scientist adds the results to his or her observations, then thinks of a new hypothesis. Good scientists admit their mistakes and wrong ideas, because their goal is to be accurate and truthful. Good science is also flexible, growing and changing as new knowledge is gained.

If the answer is "yes," the scientist usually *repeats* the experiment to make sure. To be considered scientific, the result of a test or experiment has to be able to be reproduced. Scientists *share* their work by publishing it in **scientific journals** so that others can repeat the experiments and learn from the results.

The scientific method is a powerful way to learn about the world. It gives scientists everywhere a clear set of standards to meet. It is also an excellent tool for identifying **pseudoscience**.

Pseudoscience

Pseudo (SOO-doh) at the beginning of a word means "false" or "fake." Pseudoscience is false science. It is presented as if it was scientific, but it does not meet the standards of good science.

Many pseudoscientific claims are not testable. For example, if someone said, "Two thousand years ago, powerful aliens moved Earth away from the center of the universe," we would have no way to test that claim. No one can produce a time machine that could take us back two thousand years to look for Earth-moving aliens, and no one can produce an alien who could answer questions about it.

Other claims may be so broad or vague that they have no meaning. "Crystals have healing power" is an example of a vague pseudoscientific claim. A scientist examining that claim would ask, "What kind of crystals? Are diamonds better for healing than plain old rock quartz? What medical conditions are crystals supposed to heal?"

Pseudoscientific claims are sometimes presented as facts, but with no evidence, or with poor evidence. If there *is* evidence, it may be statistics or quotes with no **sources**. Without knowing exactly where a piece of information comes from, it's impossible to check that the source is reliable and the information is accurate. The scientist researching the claim about crystals would want to know, "Has this claim been tested in hospitals and laboratories? What were the

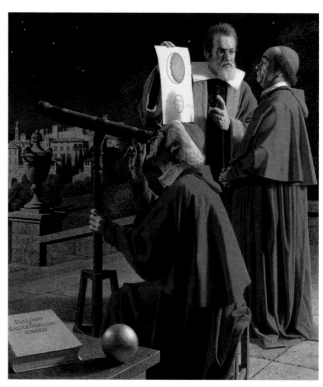

Galileo demonstrates his work. He was the first to make important observations of the heavens using a new tool: the telescope.

Science or Pseudoscience?

FEATURES OF SCIENCE:

- Based on scientific method

- Uses reason and logic

- Looks for physical forces to
  explain results

- Testable

- Results can be reproduced

- Published in scientific journals, and
  for the general public, too

FEATURES OF PSEUDOSCIENCE:

- Often based on tradition or folklore

- Appeals to feelings

- Explains results in mystical or mysterious ways

- May not be testable

- Results cannot be regularly reproduced

- Published for the general public,
  sometimes does not meet standards of
  scientific journals

results? Have those results been published in scientific journals?"

Finally, pseudoscience is often based on beliefs and feelings rather than logic and reason. A pseudoscientific idea may spring from tradition, folklore, or even religious writings. However, the fact that an idea, claim, or belief is pseudoscience does not always mean that the idea cannot possibly be true. It only means that it is not science.

The scientific method has cast light on many mysteries and answered many questions. Four hundred years ago, in Galileo's time, one of the most serious questions was whether Earth moves through space. Long before Galileo, though, a few thinkers had asked that very question.

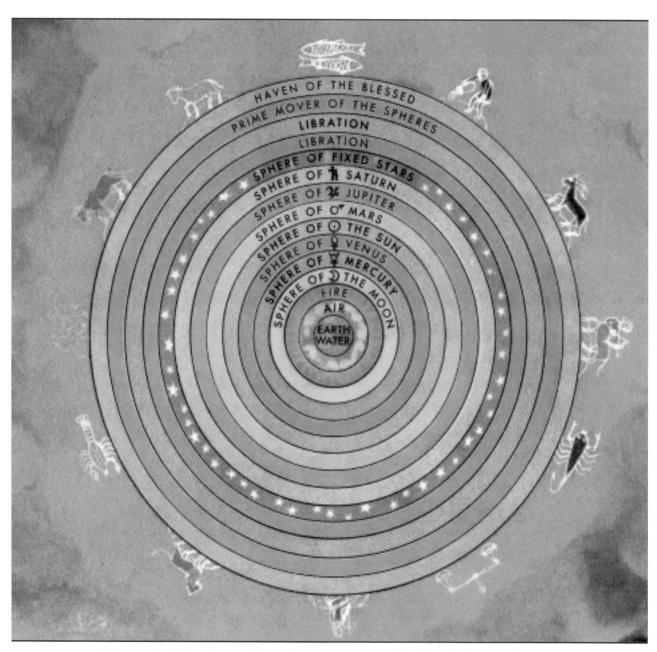

The ancient Greeks saw the universe as a set of hollow balls, or spheres, around Earth. In some versions, the moon and sun were closest to Earth. In this view, Mercury and Venus are closer than the sun.

TWO

Circles and More Circles

Astronomers in ancient China kept detailed records of the positions of the stars and the movements of the planets, as did many other civilizations. The first questions about Earth's own position and movement came from ancient Greece.

The Earth-Centered Universe

The ancient Greeks, like other cultures, thought that Earth was at the center of the universe and that the sun, moon, planets, and stars revolved around it. Most of them also believed that Earth stood completely still. A few of them claimed that Earth rotated on its axis.

Picture a straight line running through Earth from the North to the South Pole, sticking out into space on each end. That is Earth's axis. Rotation means spinning around in place. If you stuck a pencil through a foam ball, stood the pencil on end on a table, and then spun the ball around, it would be rotating on its axis.

Almost everyone—including those who thought Earth rotated—pictured the universe as geocentric. Two of ancient Greece's most famous thinkers, Plato and Aristotle, who lived in the 4th century BC, described the Earth-centered universe this way:

Earth was a round body, or sphere, fixed at the center of the universe. The heavenly bodies were attached to larger, hollow, invisible spheres that enclosed Earth at different distances. Closest to Earth was the sphere of the moon. Then came the sun, Mercury, Venus, Mars, Jupiter, Saturn, and finally the stars. Each of these spheres rotated, or spun, at a different speed. As the spheres spun, the heavenly bodies attached to them revolved around Earth.

Ptolemy, pictured with the goddess Astronomia.

A century after Plato and Aristotle, a Greek mathematician and astronomer known as Aristarchus of Samos became the first person—as far as we know today—to offer a different model of the universe. In his model, Earth revolved around the sun. The sun, not Earth, was the fixed point at the center of the sphere of stars.

The Parallax Problem

One reason Aristarchus's idea of a heliocentric or sun-centered universe did not catch on was the parallax problem. If Earth moved around the sun, then the stars' positions should appear different at different times of the year because of the parallax effect.

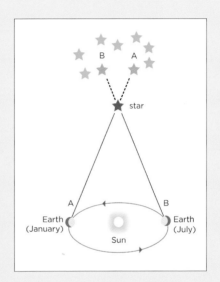

This diagram shows how parallax would change the position of the red star as seen from Earth, if Earth revolved around the sun. In January, the red star would be at point A in the sky. In July, it would be at point B. But neither Aristarchus nor any other astronomer of his time saw a single star shift its position.

Aristarchus correctly explained the lack of parallax by saying that the stars were much farther away than anyone had thought, making the parallax shifts tiny and impossible to see with current tools. Other astronomers, however, were not convinced. They stuck with the geocentric view.

Ptolemy and "The Greatest"

Ptolemy was an astronomer, geographer, and mathematician who lived in Alexandria, Egypt, in the second century AD. He tackled the issue of how the universe was arranged in an astronomical book that became known as the *Almagest*, which is Arabic for "The Greatest."

Ptolemy was indeed the greatest astronomer of his time. His model of the universe became so well known in later centuries that it is sometimes called the Ptolemaic model. Although Ptolemy was not the first to develop this view of the universe, he worked it out in great detail.

The Ptolemaic model was geocentric. The closest body to revolve around Earth was the moon, followed by Mercury, Venus, the sun, and the stars.

This medieval chart of the heavens used Ptolemy's ideas, with the sun and planets revolving around Earth.

But the retrograde movements of the planets gave astronomers trouble. They felt that the planets must move around Earth
in perfect circles. Why, then, did the planets periodically drift
"backward" against the stars? The solution was more circles:
smaller ones called **epicycles**.

In this model, each planet traveled around and around a small circle called an epicycle. The center of each epicycle traveled around Earth on a larger circle called a deferent. (Today we would call it an orbit.) Technically, the planets didn't revolve around Earth—their epicycles did.

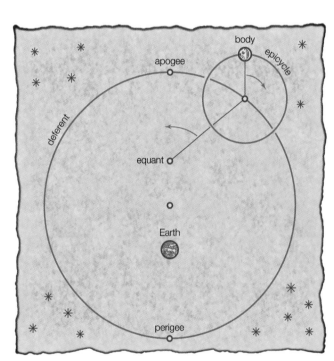

Ptolemy took this model and expanded on it. He was a very good observer of the heavens and had an accurate understanding of the planets' positions and movements. He realized that a plain geocentric

**To make the Earth-centered scheme work,
astronomers claimed that the planets revolved
in small circles while those circles revolved
around Earth.**

model, or even a geocentric model with one epicycle for each
planet, could not account for all those movements. To make the
model fit his observations, Ptolemy added more and more epicycles, until the Ptolemaic universe became extremely complicated.

Ptolemy never did completely solve the problem of explaining the planets' movements with epicycles. He died around 180 AD. The Arab scholars who built upon his work centuries later were some of the best astronomers and mathematicians in the world, but for the most part they remained tied to Ptolemy's geocentric view of the universe. The first real challenges to geocentrism did not come until the sixteenth century.

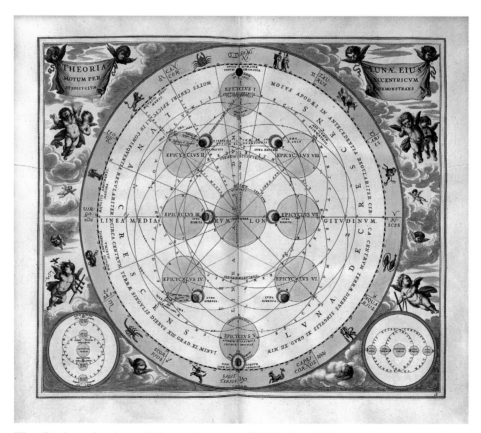

The Ptolemaic view of the universe, with Earth at the center, required more and more epicycles (small circular orbits) to explain the movements of the planets.

New Views and a New Tool

Around 1440 a German priest and mathematician named Nicholas of Cusa suggested that Earth might not be the center of the universe after all. A few decades later, an Indian astronomer named Nilakantha Somayaji developed a variation on geocentrism. Earth was still at the center, with the sun revolving around it, but Somayaji thought that the planets revolved around the sun. His work influenced Indian astronomers but remained unknown in Europe. During the sixteenth century, the heliocentric revolution really got rolling in Europe with the work of a Polish churchman and astronomer, Nicolaus Copernicus.

Too Many Epicycles!

When Copernicus considered the universe, he became convinced that the Ptolemaic system must be wrong. Not only did it fail to account completely for all the planetary movements that astronomers observed, it had become ridiculously complicated.

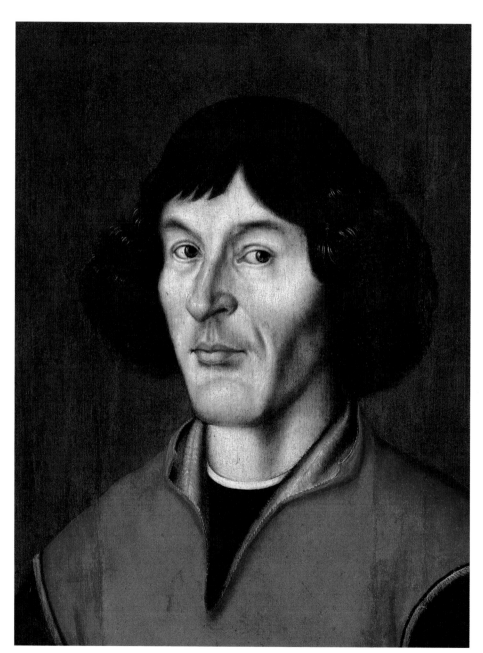

Nicolaus Copernicus (1473-1543) offered a bold new idea: Earth moves around the sun.

The Ptolemaic model creaked and groaned under the weight of epicycles upon epicycles.

Copernicus came up with a hypothesis for a simpler, more accurate system. His hypothesis was this: the sun, not Earth, is the center of the heavens. In Copernicus's heliocentric system, the planets Mercury, Venus, Earth, Mars, Jupiter, and Saturn revolved around the sun in circular orbits. The moon revolved around Earth.

Once he began testing this hypothesis by comparing it with

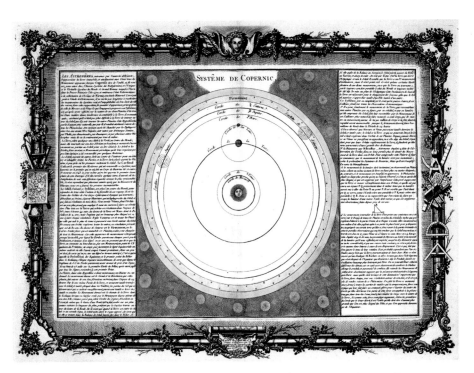

A 1761 illustration of Copernicus's heliocentric system shows the sun at the center, Earth revolving around the sun, and the moon revolving around Earth.

measurements of the planetary movements, he saw that his heliocentric model, with Earth and all the planets revolving around the sun, solved the retrograde problem.

The solution worked this way:

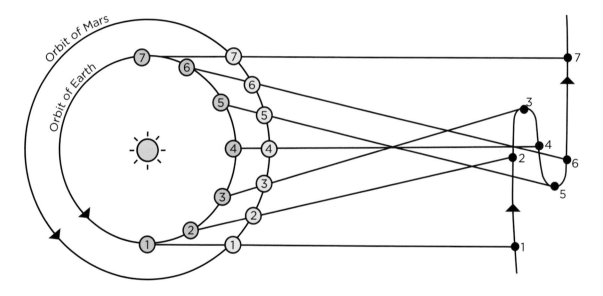

As seen from Earth, Mars sometimes appears to move backward in its orbit.

As Earth and Mars move around the sun in their different orbits, Earth periodically catches up with Mars, and then passes it. As seen from Earth, the path of Mars appears to make a loop in the sky. At last—a satisfactory explanation of retrograding!

The Copernican model was starting to look like the solar system as we know it today. However, it had several serious problems. One problem was that the system still did not quite account for all the movements of the planets. To do that, Copernicus found himself adding epicycles—the very problem he had tried to escape. Still, his model remained simpler and more accurate than any that had come before it. A different problem concerned how people would react when their view of the universe was challenged.

The Roman Catholic Church wielded enormous power at that time. Church authorities had the power to imprison, torture, and even kill people who promoted ideas that the church considered dangerous because they went against its established teachings. The geocentric model of the universe was one of the church's established teachings because some Bible verses mention the sun moving and Earth being fixed in place. Ideas like Copernicus's could lead to serious trouble with the church.

By 1533, Copernicus had recorded his heliocentric ideas. Some friends and fellow scholars, including an archbishop, read his book and urged him to publish it, but he hesitated. *De Revolutionibus Orbium Celestium*, meaning "On the Revolutions of the Heavenly Bodies," was finally published in 1543, just days before Copernicus died at the age of seventy. Only a few scholars spoke up in support of it, but the Copernican heliocentric idea had been let loose upon the world.

No More Perfect Circles

The next link in the scientific chain that led from geocentrism to heliocentrism was Johannes Kepler, a German astronomer. Kepler set out to test Copernicus's idea that Earth revolved around the sun.

Kepler had one great advantage. In 1601 he inherited a mass of highly accurate observations made over many years by Tycho Brahe, a Danish astronomer with whom he had worked for several years. With this data at hand, it didn't matter that Kepler's eyesight was too weak for him to make his own observations. He set to work studying the movements of the planets, especially Mars, as Tycho had recorded them.

Planetary movements, Kepler decided, were better explained by a heliocentric solar system than by a geocentric one. Still, the heliocentric model did not quite fit. At last Kepler found a hypothesis that explained the planets' movements. Their orbits around the sun were not perfect circles, as everyone had always thought. They were ellipses, or ovals. The planet's movements fit the heliocentric system perfectly if their orbits were pictured as almost circular, but not quite. Kepler's greatest contribution to astronomy was making this small but important adjustment to the Copernican model.

Galileo's Vision

Astronomy changed forever at the beginning of the seventeenth century, after Dutch spectacle-makers invented the telescope.

Johannes Kepler (left), discovered that the orbits of the planets
are not circular. Punished by the church, Galileo (right) received an
apology from Pope John Paul II 359 years later, in 1992.

This simple arrangement of several lenses in a tube made distant
objects appear larger and closer.

At first people saw the telescope as a way to see faraway
things on Earth, such as mountains and ships, in detail. But in
1609, an English scientist named Thomas Harriot turned one of
the new instruments skyward. He made the first known astronomical observation through a telescope, comparing the surface
of a full moon to a pie.

That same year, Italian mathematician and scientist Galileo Galilei built the first of many telescopes he would use over the years. Galileo already thought that Copernicus's theory of the solar system was correct. What he saw through his telescopes made a strong case for the truth of heliocentrism.

The planet Jupiter had its own moons revolving around it—proof that not everything in the solar system revolved around Earth. By itself, this fact did not prove heliocentrism, but it disproved geocentrism. Stronger evidence of heliocentrism came from Galileo's observations of the planet Venus.

Seen through a telescope, Venus showed phases like those of the moon: crescent, half full, full, and dark. But Venus could only appear full (that is, with its whole surface bright and illuminated) to an observer on Earth if it were on the opposite side of the sun from Earth. Since Venus does sometimes appear full to observers on Earth, it must sometimes be on the other side of the sun from Earth. This could not happen in the Ptolemaic system, because in that system, Venus and the sun were both supposed to orbit Earth, with the sun farther out than Venus. If this were true, the sun could never get between Earth and Venus—and Venus could never be full as seen from Earth. Instead, Galileo's observations strongly suggested that Venus and Earth both orbit the sun, with Venus closer to the sun than Earth.

To Galileo, the phases of Venus were a strong proof of heliocentrism. Some other astronomers were not convinced. They also pointed out that even with a telescope Galileo had not seen a star appear to shift because of the parallax effect, which would be an even stronger proof of the Earth's movement. Galileo, however, continued to write about and defend the Copernican system. In 1616, he traveled to Rome to ask the church not to ban Copernicus's work. Church authorities told him that heliocentrism was false and warned him not to promote it as a fact.

Sixteen years later, Galileo thought that things had changed. The pope and head of the church, Urban VIII, had been a friend and an admirer of his work. He encouraged Galileo to publish a book outlining the arguments for and against the geocentric and heliocentric systems. He also warned Galileo to remain neutral and not take the side of heliocentrism.

Unfortunately, when Galileo's *Dialogue Concerning the Two Chief World Systems* was published, it offended the pope. Urban thought Galileo had made the geocentric view—the pope's own view—look foolish. He also felt that the book clearly supported heliocentrism. In 1633 Galileo was summoned to Rome to stand trial in a church court. Under threat of torture, he was forced to declare that the theory that Earth moves around the sun was false.

Galileo spent the rest of his life under house arrest. His books were banned. Still, he had advanced heliocentrism in two ways: by testing the sun-centered theory with mathematics and by using a new scientific tool, the telescope, to learn more about the planets than had ever been known before.

four

The Sun-Centered Solar System

By the end of the seventeenth century, heliocentrism was known across Europe. It was accepted by most scientists, and by 1758, even the church was ready to remove books that mentioned heliocentrism from its "forbidden reading" list.

Isaac Newton (1642-1727)

One important piece of the heliocentric picture was filled in by English scientist Isaac Newton in 1687 when he published a book known as the *Principia*, or "Principles." Newton described gravity as the force that gives matter weight and makes it attract other matter. As Newton showed, the gravitational force of the Earth and moon, acting together, keeps the moon orbiting around Earth instead of flying off into space. Gravity causes the heavenly bodies to behave as they do. Before Newton, astronomers knew that the planets revolve around the sun. After Newton, they knew *why*.

The Solar System Today

In 1781 something happened that had never occurred in all of history: a new planet was added to the solar system. Uranus, visible only through a telescope, was discovered beyond the orbit of Saturn. In time, astronomers became puzzled by Uranus. Its orbit did not follow the path that it should have, according to the laws of planetary motion.

Astronomers tackled the problem using the scientific method. One promising hypothesis was that an unknown planet, even farther from the sun than Uranus, was pulling on Uranus with gravitational force. To test that hypothesis, researchers used mathematics to figure out where the unknown planet should be, and then used telescopes to search the sky for it. In 1846, they found Neptune, the eighth planet in the solar system.

The solar system as we know it today contains even more bodies: dwarf planets such as Pluto and Eris, belts of asteroids and small icy worlds, and clouds of comets. More than 140 moons orbit the planets and dwarf planets, with more moons discovered all the time. And all of the planets, dwarf planets, asteroids, and comets revolve around the sun, just as Aristarchus suggested several thousand years ago . . . although he could not have dreamed there would be so many of them!

A Universe in Motion

Geocentrists did not just believe that the heavenly bodies moved around Earth. They also believed that Earth did not move at all. The movements of Earth are now well understood, however.

The Earth rotates, or spins, at a speed of about 1,000 miles an hour measured at the equator. It travels on its orbit around the sun at approximately 67,000 miles an hour. And although the sun is at the center of our solar system, it does not stand still. The sun and the entire solar system are revolving around the center of the Milky Way galaxy, the huge group of billions of stars that is our "neighborhood" in space. Traveling at a speed of about 500,000 miles an hour, the sun takes more than 200 million years to complete one revolution around the galaxy.

The Parallax Problem Solved

One reason Tycho Brahe did not accept heliocentrism was that no one had seen stellar parallax, the shift of a star's position against the background. If Earth was really moving, stars should show the parallax effect. Other astronomers thought that the stars were simply too far away for their parallax shifts to be measured. Finally, in 1838, thanks to advances in telescopes, a German astronomer named Friedrich Bessel became the first to measure stellar parallax when he observed the star 61 Cygni from different points along Earth's orbit.

Materials have changed, but a replica of Newton's seventeenth-century telescope (top) has a lot in common with a modern small telescope (bottom). Both are tubes that contain lenses to magnify the object being viewed. Mirrors reflect the magnified image into an eyepiece (the small tube sticking out on the side of the telescope) so that the astronomer can see it clearly.

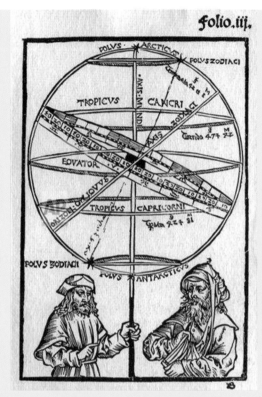

folio.iij.

An armillary sphere is a model of objects in the sky as seen from Earth. That's why Earth is in the center of the sphere, although not at the center of the universe.

Is Geocentrism Alive?

The famous detective Sherlock Holmes was a genius but an unusual one. He knew a lot about crime but was strangely ignorant about some other subjects. One sign of his strangeness was that he didn't know, or care, whether Earth revolved around the sun or the sun revolved around Earth. But Sherlock Holmes was a fictional creation. What about real people?

Heliocentrism is not yet universally known or accepted. In a 1999 poll, 18 percent of Americans said that the sun revolves around Earth, while 79 percent said Earth revolves around the sun. Four years later, in a different poll, only 71 percent of Americans agreed that Earth revolves around the sun. Confusion about the solar system is not limited to the United States. A 2011 poll found that 32 percent of Russians think the sun revolves around Earth.

Like Sherlock Holmes, some people simply do not know or care whether the solar system is geocentric or heliocentric. A few people argue passionately for geocentrism. A group led by Catholics who believe in an Earth-centered universe has even organized conferences on the subject "Galileo Was Wrong: The Church Was Right." Although they maintain that geocentrism is supported by science, their views have so far appeared only in their own blogs and publications, not in scientific journals.

Uranus, the first planet discovered through a telescope, has a ring system like that of Saturn's.

Even galaxies move. Astronomers now think that all of the billions of galaxies in the universe are flying apart from each other as the universe grows larger and larger. The Earth's motion around the sun may seem tiny in the midst of this vast movement, but heliocentrism, a triumph of scientific discovery, led to our ever-growing understanding of the universe.

Glossary

astronomer	a scientist who studies space and the things in it
astronomy	the scientific study of space and the things in it
epicycle	a small circle in which the center moves around in the circumference of a larger circle
geocentric	having Earth in the center
geocentrism	the belief or idea that Earth is the center of the solar system or universe
heliocentric	having the sun in the center
heliocentrism	the belief or idea that the sun is the center of the solar system or universe
orbit	the path followed by an object moving through space

parallax   the appearance of movement in a distant object when it is seen from different viewpoints

pseudoscience   false science; something that looks like science, or claims to be science, but isn't

retrograde   movement backward, as when a planet seen from Earth appears to move back along its path for a while and then move forward again

revolve   to move around something else; one full time around is a revolution

rotate   to spin around, the way a top spins; one spin is a rotation

scientific journal a magazine with articles written by scientists; before appearing in a journal, an article must be approved as scientific by a panel of experts (this is called peer review)

scientific method a set of practical steps for answering questions about the world and adding to knowledge

solar system a sun and all the planets, moons, comets, asteroids, and other bodies that revolve around it

source details about where a piece of information comes from, so that others can check to see whether the source is reliable and the information is repeated accurately

zodiac a band or zone in the heavens along the path that the sun appears to follow over the course of a year; the moon and planets are also always within the zodiac

Timeline

388 BC	Greek Philosopher Plato teaches that heavenly bodies circle Earth
270 BC	Aristarchus of Samus proposes a heliocentric, or sun-centered, universe
150 AD	Claudius Ptolemaeus (Ptolemy) writes about the geocentric, or earth-centered universe; his model is used for 1,500 years
ca. 1440	Nicolas of Cusa suggests that Earth might not be the center of the universe
ca. 1500	Nilakantha Somyaji suggests that the sun revolves around Earth, but the planets revolve around the sun
1543	Nicolaus Copernicus publishes a book about the heliocentric universe
1601	Thomas Harriot makes the first known observation of the heavens using a telescope; Johannes Kepler inherits data about the

	movements of the planets from astronomer Tycho Brahe
1609	Johannes Kepler explains that the planets' orbits are elliptical, not circular
1609–1632	Galileo Galilei builds his own telescopes and supports a heliocentric view, offending the pope
1633	The Catholic Church forces Galileo to declare his theory false
1687	Issac Newton describes gravity as it relates to the movements of heavenly bodies
1781	William Herschel, using a telescope, discovers a new planet, Uranus
1838	Friedrich Bessel measures stellar parallax, proving that Earth moves
1846	Astronomers discover the planet Neptune
1992	The Catholic Church admits it issued the wrong verdict in Galileo's trial

Find Out More

Books

Aguilar, David A. *13 Planets: The Latest View of the Solar System*. Des Moines, IA: National Geographic Children's Books, 2011.

Andronik, Catherine M. *Copernicus: Founder of Modern Astronomy*. Rev. ed. Berkeley Heights, NJ: Enslow, 2009.

Carey, Stephen S. *A Beginner's Guide to Scientific Method*. Independence, KY: Wadsworth, 2011.

Chown, Marcus. *Solar System: A Visual Exploration of All the Planets, Moons, and Other Heavenly Bodies that Orbit Our Sun*. New York: Black Dog & Leventhal, 2011.

Gianopolous, Andrea. *Isaac Newton and the Laws of Motion*. Oxford, UK: Raintree, 2007.

Glass, Susan. *Prove It! The Scientific Method in Action*. Oxford, UK: Raintree, 2006.

Hasan, Heather. *Kepler and the Laws of Planetary Motion*. Berkeley Heights, NJ: Enslow, 2005.

Kerrod, Robin. *Universe.* New York: DK Children's, 2009.

Miles, Lisa, Alastair Smith, and Judy Tatchell. *The Usborne Book of Astronomy and Space.* London: Usborne, 2010.

Mitton, Jacqueline. *Galileo: Scientist and Star Gazer.* New York: Oxford University Press, 2009.

Nardo, Don. *Tycho Brahe: Pioneer of Astronomy.* Mankato, MN: Compass Point, 2008.

Steele, Philip. *Galileo: The Genius Who Faced the Inquisition.* Des Moines, IA: National Geographic Children's Books, 2008.

Websites

The History of Astronomy
http://curious.astro.cornell.edu/history.php
Cornell University's "Curious About Astronomy?" website has a page about the history of astronomy, with links to articles about the discovery that the Earth moves around the sun.

How Science Works
http://kids.niehs.nih.gov/explore/scienceworks/index.htm

Part of the National Institute of Health website, How Science Works is designed for kids and includes a summary of the scientific method.

PBS.org
Galileo's Battle for the Heavens
http://www.pbs.org/wgbh/nova/ancient/galileo-battle-for-the-heavens.html
This PBS site links to a Nova program that explores Galileo's life and work, focusing on his realization that Earth orbits the sun. Includes links to related websites.

Bibliography

The author found these sources especially helpful in researching this book. A complete list of sources is on her website, www.rebeccastefoff.com, under Sources>Earth or Sun.

Butterworth, Paul and David Palmer. "Speed of the Earth's Rotation." **NASA's Imagine the Universe**. Last modified April 1, 1997. http://imagine.gsfc.nasa.gov/docs/ask_astro/answers/970401c.html.

Cowell, Alan. "After 350 Years, Vatican Says Galileo Was Right: It Moves." *New York Times*. October 31, 1992. www.nytimes.

com/1992/10/31/world/after-350-years-vatican-says-galileo-was-right-it-moves.html?src=pm.

Crabtree, Steve. "New Poll Gauges Americans' General Knowledge Levels." **Gallup News Service**. July 6, 1999. http://www.gallup.com/poll/3742/new-poll-gauges-americans-general-knowledge-levels.aspx.

De Carbonnel, Alissa. "Does the sun revolve around the Earth? One in every three Russians thinks so." **Reuters News Service**. February 11, 2011. http://uk.reuters.com/article/2011/02/11/science-us-russia-poll-education-science-idUKTRE-71A5B920110211.

Galilei, Galileo. *The Essential Galileo*. Edited by Maurice Finocchiaro. Indianapolis, IN: Hackett, 2008.

Gingerich, Owen. *The Eye of Heaven: Ptolemy, Copernicus, Kepler*. New York: American Institute of Physics, 1993.

Hofstadter, Dan. *The Earth Moves: Galileo and the Roman Inquisition*. New York: Norton, 2010.

Khan, Razid. "Who thinks the sun goes around the Earth?" *Discover*. March 28, 2011. http://blogs.discovermagazine.com/

gnxp/2011/03/who-thinks-the-sun-goes-around-the-earth.

Moran, Andrew. "Conservative Catholics say Galileo was wrong, geocentric is right." **Digital Journal**. August 29, 2011. Online at http://digitaljournal.com/article/310901.

Plait, Phil. "Geocentrism? Seriously?" *Discover*. September 14, 2010. http://blogs.discovermagazine.com/badastronomy/2010/09/14/geocentrism-seriously/

Sobel, Dava. *A More Perfect Heaven: How Copernicus Revolutionized the Cosmos*. New York: Walker, 2011.

Sungenis, Robert. *Galileo Was Wrong: The Church Was Right*. 3 vols. State Line, PA: Catholic Apologetics International Publishing, 2007.

Vollmann, William T. *Uncentering the Earth: Copernicus and the Revolution of the Heavenly Spheres*. New York: Norton, 2007.

Index

About the Author

Rebecca Stefoff has written many books for young readers on a variety of subjects: science, exploration, history, literature, and biography. Her books about science include the four-volume series Animal Behavior Revealed, numerous books about animals and biology, and a biography of Charles Darwin. She has also probed the mysteries of the unexplained in the five-volume series Secrets of the Supernatural (Marshall Cavendish Benchmark, 2008). Stefoff lives in Portland, Oregon, where she likes to peer at the night sky through her telescope when the clouds break.